DAILY THOUGHTS FOR THE LENTEN JOURNEY

He will be gracious to you as you journey.
He will hear your cry.
When he hears, he will answer.

When the Lord has given you the bread of suffering
and the water of distress,
he who is your teacher will hide no longer
and you will see him with your own eyes.

When you turn to right or to left on your journey
your ears will hear these words behind you:
'This is the way, follow it.'

Isaiah 30:19-21

Niall Ahern

Daily thoughts for the Lenten Journey

First published in 2012 by
the columba press
55A Spruce Avenue, Stillorgan Industrial Park,
Blackrock, Co Dublin

Designed by Bill Bolger

The cover picture is *The Pilgrim Journey* sculpture from the North-west Transept, Cathedral of the Immaculate Conception, Sligo.
The illustrations in this book are by Sóirle Mac Cana, and are taken from *Irish Craftsmanship* (Irish Hospitals' Trust, 1940), and are used by permission.
Origination by The Columba Press
Printed in Ireland by Turner's Printing Ltd, Longford.

ISBN 978-1-85607-764-4

Acknowledgements
These reflections by Niall Ahern, which have been delivered as radio talks over the past few years, are adapted from Tom Cox's Intercom liturgical cycle of Scripture Thoughts, which is to be published soon. We hope this compendium will bring focus and encouragement to all our Lenten readers.

Contents

Foreword by *Baroness Nuala O'Loan* 7
Introduction 9
Lenten Prayer 11

Season of Lent 13
Ash Wednesday 14
Thursday after Ash Wednesday 16
Friday after Ash Wednesday 18
Saturday after Ash Wednesday 19

First Week of Lent 21
Sunday 22
Monday 23
Tuesday 24
Wednesday 26
Thursday 27
Friday 28
Saturday 29

Second Week of Lent 31
Sunday 32
Monday 33
Tuesday 34
Wednesday 35
Thursday 36
Friday 38
Saturday 39

Third Week of Lent 41
Sunday 42
Monday 43
Tuesday 44

Wednesday 45
Thursday 46
Friday 47
Saturday 48

Fourth Week of Lent 49
Sunday 50
Monday 52
Tuesday 53
Wednesday 54
Thursday 55
Friday 56
Saturday 57

Fifth Week of Lent 59
Sunday 60
Monday 62
Tuesday 64
Wednesday 66
Thursday 67
Friday 69
Saturday 70

Holy Week 73
Palm Sunday 74
Monday 75
Tuesday 77
Spy Wednesday 79
Holy Thursday 81
Good Friday 83
Holy Saturday 85

Easter Sunday 87

Foreword

Lent is a time of waiting. It is full of expectation and hope of resurrection. But all of this is preceded by pain and suffering and darkness. We journey for forty days with a certain heaviness and lived uncertainty. Lent invites us to enter more deeply into the mystery of our faith. The mystery Christ himself lived. The mystery we experience unfolding before our very own eyes as we traverse the Lenten road.

It is a consolation to be accompanied; it is good to know we are not alone; it is helpful to have someone place signposts on our path and Niall Ahern in his Radio Reflections last year assures us that God walks by our side. When we quietly listened each day to his compelling words we found revealed in sharp relief the difficult, challenging and sometimes overwhelming realities we live. The realities from which we cannot escape. The reality of passion on our journey. But the reality of God's presence was there too.

Quite simply, and in an attuned yet gently straightforward manner, Niall speaks to us about the ordinary nature of the Lenten journey. As we contemplate his words we find he encourages us with compelling conviction to believe that our Gethsemane, our Calvary, our Cross is part of our ongoing journey into God.

God is the one for whom we wait as we make the Lenten journey and it is good that these *Daily Thoughts for the Lenten Journey* are now in book form so that we can return to them when our spirits are low or we fear we may have lost our way. Each day, through these reflections, we are made more aware of how intimately Jesus experienced God's desire in this regard as he journeyed. We realise that every small step can be a journey of discovery, of disclosure and ultimately of resurrection.

Perhaps the question which Niall presents us with here is not so much what Lent is about as what we individually are about as we live each prosaic day of this season and discover God's hidden and as yet unrevealed word for each one of us.

This is an urgent journey; it is a necessary journey; it is a worthwhile journey. There is full reason to believe it will also be a blessed journey.

Baroness Nuala O'Loan

Introduction

Any day is a good day to journey into God. Ash Wednesday is the first day of Lent and a good day to start this journey. We have long stretches of days ahead of us before we reach Easter. It is a great opportunity, a chance to develop our thoughts about the passion, instead of trying to fit them into the gaps between last minute Easter preparations at the end of Holy Week. But it is quite a long time to remain resolute in looking daily at the small, irksome, challenging details of our life's pattern. That is what this journey is all about – the daily meeting with God in the ordinary steps of each day.

'Who are you looking for?' That is the Easter question and the answer is to be found in the long haul of daily living. The answer is Jesus, risen and alive. We probe the question differently here by asking ourselves for each of the forthcoming forty days 'What is Lent about?' And while it is about drudgery and tiredness and road weariness it is ultimately about resurrection, about Jesus risen and alive.

Let us start the journey in silence. In attentive waiting with an attuned ear for the nuances of God's presence in the simplest detail of life's journey. Let it be a listening journey, a prayerful wander through mystery to new vision.

Silence is so close to prayer that we can almost say silence is prayer. It can be the silence of mutual enjoyment, when we are in the presence of God without needing to say a word. Or it can be the silence of accepted suffering, when we do not tense up against the pain, but open ourselves in an act of self-giving. It is such silence that is Jesus' silence now – the silence in which he gathers all his faculties into an act of tranquil self-giving to God.

Lent is about tranquil self-giving, so let the journey begin!

Niall Ahern

Lenten Prayer

God, our Father,
through the power of the Holy Spirit,
you sent your Son,
Jesus Christ,
to lead us from death to life,
sin to pardon.

As we prepare this Lent
to share in this passion and death,
open our heart to the wonder
of his Resurrection.

Heal our wounds.
Bless our endeavours.
And as we commence this journey,
make us gentle of heart.

Amen.

Season of Lent

TOP LEFT: Ornamental initial and lettering from the *Book of Kells*.
TOP RIGHT: An ornamental circle showing Spiral and Trumpet pattern from the page preceding the Epistle of St Jerome, *Book of Durrow*.
CENTRE: One of the symbols of the Four Evangelists, the Eagle (St John) from the *Book of Kells*.
BACK RIGHT: Ornamental panel from the *Lindisfarne Gospels*.

Ash Wednesday

Today is Ash Wednesday, the first day of Lent, the beginning of the wilderness test.

The wilderness test starts with the ashes on our foreheads. At some point in our life, we have to go into the desert to identify what compulsions operate in our lives. It can begin at any stage in our lives. It may come when your second parent has died, when you realise that you are no longer someone's son or daughter, but an individual standing alone on the surface of life. Whenever it comes, you have to go into the desert to stare your inner chaos in the face. Face the demons, they don't change that much with age.

Ash Wednesday reminds us of our demons, so stand with them today even if you are alone. There is the demon of grandiosity. It tells us that we are the centre of the universe, that our lives are more important than those of others. Loneliness is a demon, as well as being the most frequently 'googled' word in Ireland. There is a demon of fear which torments us by telling us constantly that at the end of the day we will all be alone, unloved, excluded, outside the circle. We look for anything or anyone to remove that fear, in the right and the wrong places. There is the demon called paranoia, which enters whenever we become embittered or cynical or distressed or angry or jealous, believing that life has cheated us, that others win and we lose.

The season of Lent has begun. It is a time to honestly confront the demons within us; to let God be God and do battle within us. This Lent let us face our demons and let us do it with the sign of the ashes on our foreheads, this day and for the forty days ahead in this Holy Season.

Amen.

Thursday after Ash Wednesday

Lent has just begun and it is about kind words and good echoes.

Kindness doesn't get much place nowadays. We live in times of shrill headlines, multichannel TV and black and white sound bites. We have long memories for past faults, but kindness has a longer memory, particularly where people are humiliated.

People may have put everything: energy, time and all their family's money into a business and then lost it all ... humiliation. Spouses are dumped, abandoned, the humiliation of being replaced. Someone is humiliated at the wrong end of a jealousy that becomes public. It is not easy to rebuild a future, regardless of whether you have been the architect or the victim of your own demise.

Perhaps we complicated religion too much with excessive rules and judges and law. Have we missed the essence? Do we see kindness and compassion as weak and empty and sneer at people with a bit of give in them? We risk forgetting that Christianity is about kindness and her close sister, compassion. We know it's what matters because it's what we remember. A kind word, a compassionate gesture, a helping hand in time of need is unforgettable and more likely to change behaviour when needed.

The Samaritan woman, whose name we don't even know from the Lenten gospels, experienced all of this, but she didn't experience a let down from the Lord. What she experienced was a lesson of compassion from one who didn't even look up to eyeball chastened accusers as they slipped away. Does she remember her accusers? We don't know, but we are sure that she remembered the Lord. Kindness always makes for lasting memories. Let that echo in your heart on this Lenten journey.

Amen.

Friday after Ash Wednesday

Lent is about pain and promise.

Some people will remember a young woman called Margaret Lawrence who perished a few years ago one early December day on the slopes of Croagh Patrick while attempting to climb the Holy Mountain three times in pilgrimage for her sick niece. For a twenty-nine-year-old she had achieved a lot, she had crossed the boundaries between the settled community and travellers, disabled and temporarily able and had the rare quality of radiating love to everyone, particularly in the special school she worked in.

This Lent we turn to another mountain, a different name, location and time to be sure, but the essentials are the same between Tabor and Croagh Patrick. A mountain and climbers ascending, often into a mist-shrouded summit and future, with the promise of a view that will seep away the pain of the ascent. Soon Christ and his closest companions will journey to climb Mount Tabor. Like all happy moments the temptation is to stay there, particularly for Peter who wanted to let the moment linger. But we know that while we must move on, we can savour the precious memory of the simple beauty of what we have seen at the summit, as we descend down into the valley.

It's different because we are different now, for we have seen the whole picture, the promise which is there behind the pain. You travel up, it seems, to travel in, and so for you I pray: God of the heights, protect and uplift you, Christ of the depths, uphold and sustain you, Spirit of the slopes, guide and grasp you this Lent and always.

Amen.

Saturday after Ash Wednesday

Lent is about a sense of perspective.

In these times where families tend to live further apart, it is good to meet. Sadly, it is all too often at the time of a death, at the funeral of a loved one. We comment on it, saying we shouldn't wait for a funeral to bring us together. Then we go our separate ways, until, of course, the next funeral – or wedding.

Conversations at such times can be a bit bizarre. Everything from property, to the price of things, but precious little about life, living and dying. It is our secret, unnamed fear – that despite all, we will die. In our cash-rich, time-poor generation we have pushed this question to one side. We are reaching a point when we know that while poverty is bad, wealth has its responsibilities. It won't satisfy your spiritual hunger. The rootlessness and lack of meaning at the heart of so much of what we give our time to is spawning a sense of unease and disillusionment.

So, let's not be too hard on the disciples of Jesus with their internal, 'Who is the greatest?' power struggle, as they accompany him to Jerusalem and the place of crucifixion. We have all been there and we're on that journey now.

In Christ, men and women down through the centuries have found someone great enough to live for and something worth dying for. Do we? This Lent we enter into a journey where perspective is given to what is really worth living for in life and what is worth giving our lives for as we journey. Take the journey gently and you'll find a new sense of perspective.

Amen.

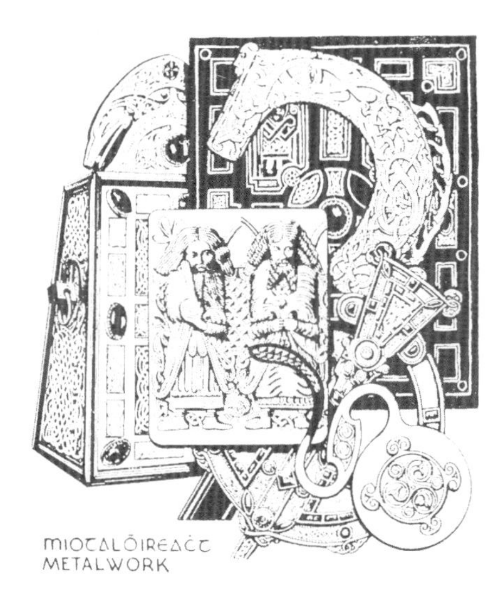

First Week of Lent

BACK LEFT: *The Shrine of St Patrick's Bell*, made in bronze, gold and silver, by Cudulig O'Inmainin and his sons.
BACK RIGHT: *The Cumdach of the Soiscél Molaise*, the Shrine of St Molaise Gospels. Made by Gilla Baithin.
IN FRONT OF SHRINE: *The Clonmacnoise Crozier*. One of the only three or four complete croziers that have survived from the Early Christian period in Ireland.
IN FRONT OF CROZIER: *The Tara Brooch*. Bronze set with panels of gold filigree, and enriched with enamels and settings of amber, blue and purple glass.
CENTRE: One of the bronze plates showing the figures of two saints in high relief from the *Breach Maedoig* or *Shrine of St Moedóg*.
LOWER RIGHT: *Bronze Hook and Disk Ornament* or *Latchet Fastener*, prepared for enamel, probably transitional. Circa fifth century, dug up at Slane, Co. Meath.

Week 1: Sunday

Lent is about keeping it light.

Who travels lightest travels furthest, is a truism. What seemed essential at the journey's beginning is discarded as soon as the shoulder straps on our rucksack begin to chaff. The general rule for packing is to lay out everything you need and take away half of it. Think, light and adaptable!

It's a truth that experienced walkers will verify. Among them the growing number of pilgrims walking the ancient Camino, or pilgrimage way, to the shrine of St. James at Santiago in Spain. They find that a long hard look at what you're packing pays off. The joy of knowing you packed blister plasters is indescribable when needed!

Maybe as we pack for a family holiday, we need to take a good look at what we are bringing with us along the road of life. We have all seen the images of people, uprooted by disaster, having to evacuate. What to bring after ourselves, food and clothing? We should hold our possessions lightly.

So, in our lives, what needs to be scrutinised and discarded? What stood us in good stead when the chips were down? Decluttering is not just about household possessions, but also attitudes and values that are unworthy of the name Christian.

Lent is a time to travel light; to leave aside the accumulated burdens of worry and resentment and striving. Light is right. Travel light this Lenten journey.

Amen.

Week 1: Monday

Lent is about words.

Many Catholics spend Lent, apart from other things, trying to refrain from using short and ugly words, but as a church we refrain from using an eight letter word. We omit the word Alleluia which we usually sing to introduce the gospel and replace it with an expression of, 'Praise to you O Christ, King of Eternal Glory' or 'Glory to you O Christ, You are the Word of God.' The word Alleluia is actually a Hebrew word meaning, 'Praise God.'

Some monastic communities took the custom a stage further. They would write the word on a scroll or a piece of paper, put it in a box and actually bury it just before Ash Wednesday. Then they would unearth it come Easter Sunday.

We don't go that far, but we should be careful not to use Alleluia during Lent in a word or in a hymn. That way, at the Easter Vigil when it is used again, it will ring out with real freshness and joy at the resurrection. We look forward to using the word, but we still have some distance to travel to Easter Day.

As the old Irish prayer says, 'Lent is a time to learn to travel, to learn to travel light. To clear the clutter from our crowded lives and find a space, a desert where there may be no joy.' Deserts are oblique places with no creature comforts and only a vast expanse of stillness. There is no Alleluia in the desert, only a sharpening awareness of ourselves and God. So, the call this Lent is just to go into the place of the desert and breath not a word until the word is Alleluia.

Amen.

Week 1: Tuesday

Lent is about forgiving and forgetting.

Apart from being an outstanding military leader during the American Civil War, speaking well of those who disliked him was one of General Robert E. Lee's notable qualities. When he paid generous tribute to the ability of a certain colleague, a fellow officer remarked, 'General, how can you speak so highly of one of our bitterest enemies, a man who never misses an opportunity to malign you?' 'My friend,' he replied, 'the President asked my opinion of him, not his opinion of me.'

Some, however, might subscribe to the words of John F. Kennedy, ironically interred in Arlington, Virginia, part of the post-Civil War confiscated estate of General Lee. He said, 'I forgive my enemies, but I never forget their names.'

Forgive and forget. Perhaps we can't forget those who hurt us, but we can do a lot to prevent it poisoning us with self-destructive hatred. The words of Jesus that we hear at this Lenten time challenge us not only to leave aside hatred, no matter how well placed and founded it may be, but also prompt us to change hatred into love. General Lee perhaps found the key to understanding this tall order of changing hatred into love. By cultivating the habit of thinking and speaking well of others, regardless of their attitude towards us, you will make an investment that will bear rich dividends for time and eternity. Paradoxically, you will bring peace to yourself and to others, as well as to a world much in need of every bit of peace that you and others can provide. It is a sign of strength rather than weakness to follow this pattern; Christ's pattern of thinking and speaking well of others. And remember today how well he is speaking of you.

Amen.

Week 1: Wednesday

Lent is about blessed wounds.

From palm branches to passion, from Hosannas to heckling, from majesty to mockery, such a Sunday is the Sunday of the Passion and it's coming soon. The events of the last weeks of Jesus' earthly life have a disconcerting familiarity, something for everyone as the unfolding events echo the seasons of the human heart.

Everyone knows pain and woundedness. Our last suppers, the imminent departures, finding we are both betrayed and betrayer in our circle. The pointless petty jealousies of wondering who is the greatest as life's greater mysteries wrap their cloak around us. So much pain and woundedness; like the parents whose newly born child's unfamiliar features mark him/her as having special needs, who surely live the truth of a Good Friday. In peace they may learn to 'behold their son' as Jesus said to his mother from the cross, but adjusting to pain takes time. There is the entombment for people buried in addiction, their families so helpless keeping vigil, wondering who will roll away the stone for us from the tomb. So much pain and woundedness, but the sounding of a note of hope by Jesus on Easter morning and taken up through the centuries by all who live in truth and love, can never be buried and shall not die but shall live.

However burdened you are, burdened with pain and wounds, keep on the Calvary road ahead this week because Easter is coming. Remain steadfast in belief, resolve, and hope and all your wounds will be blessed.

Amen.

Week 1: Thursday

Lent is about showing the marks.

Every silver item you can care to examine will bear some mark, initials or emblem placed there by the jeweller or manufacturer. These markings are called 'hallmarks' and they have that name because centuries ago all silver items whether pots, dishes, trays, utensils or jewellery were produced by a member of a guild or union who met and worked in large rooms called halls. Hallmarks are etched or engraved for two reasons. They show that the item is actually what it appears to be; that it is in fact pure quality silver. Secondly a hallmark signifies where the product comes from; what 'hall' it comes from and in some cases which individual made it.

Thinking about hallmarks can help us in facing the issues of the Lenten gospel. Take Thomas the absent disciple when Jesus first appears after the resurrection; Thomas who doubts his fellow apostles excited testimony; Thomas of the healthy scepticism. To be honest, we all want some evidence before we accept as truth whatever is told to us. We know the story. Thomas saw the hallmarks of Jesus' death, of his love, and saw them in his wounds. People still look for hallmarks in people: a life that resembles God's, a life of light and of truth and of faith. And the question really is, Are you hallmarked? Are you the genuine article?

You are, if the wounds that you bear this Lent are borne through your struggle to identify with Christ and his love: nailed with Christ, hallmarked by him for life. The genuine article. What more need be said?

Amen.

Week 1: Friday

Lent is about a door to life.

Until the channel between France and England, the longest tunnel on earth was the eleven kilometre Mont Blanc Tunnel which since 1965 links Italy and Switzerland. Anxieties ran high among its first users, some even turned back at the pleading of loved ones.

Writers of death, often depict death as a deep dark tunnel. Lazarus entered this tunnel but came out again on the same side with the same body. Eventually he got sick and died again. People mourned and buried him. Being honest, we want loved ones to live forever, for death is an uncomfortable fact. We trumpet the advances of medical science. Hardly anyone in Ireland dies of tuberculosis or polio, diphtheria or smallpox anymore and that is good news.

However, the death rate remains at a flat 100%. You can jog, avoid cholesterol, watch your health and you will still end up the healthiest corpse that ever died, because death is still the master of our race and nothing can be done about it. But someone did something about it, making death a door not a dead end; from an enemy to a friend. Like Lazarus, Jesus entered the tunnel of death, but on Easter Day Jesus came out the other side. He is our hope of resurrection. Lent is the road towards Easter Day, the narrow gate, the open door. Enter into the spirit of Lent now. Look to the new horizons, because our lives are of eternal consequence to God.

Amen.

Week 1: Saturday

Lent is about right deeds – right attitudes!

19 October 2003 saw the beatification of Mother Teresa, whose Missionaries of Charity cover the globe in their work with, and identification with, the poor. Their deeds match their words.

However, a revealing insight on the Lenten Gospels is given by one of her congregation. Attending a First World conference on the poor, she spoke at the closing session of her emotions over the previous afternoon which was left free for people to shop and relax until an evening gourmet meal. A miserable time was spent angrily watching the opulence all around and thinking of so many who had nothing. Come evening, she sat in the conference bus while the others dined. It was a long time, with many thoughts running through her head and asking the question, 'Would Jesus be in there eating and drinking and having a good time?' She had the horrible realisation that he would be, that the fault was in her, 'There was coldness inside me. I had become like the older brother of the prodigal son, doing all the right things, but having no celebration in my heart.'

Lenten fasting, as Jesus prescribes it, also includes fasting from bitterness of heart. Mellowness of heart is a non-negotiable within the spiritual life. Why? Because otherwise, like the older brother of the prodigal son, we might succumb to the temptation that T.S. Eliot describes,

'The last temptation that's the greatest treason is to do the right thing for the wrong reason.'

It is good to fast this Lent, but fast most healthily from hardness of heart so that Easter will be a feast of love.

Amen.

Second Week of Lent

TOP LEFT: *The Dalway Harp*, so called because of its association with a family of that name. It bears the date 1621 and is very elaborately carved with grotesque animal and floral ornament. Upon it are the names of those for whom it was made as well as that of the craftsman who produced it, Donnachad FitzTeige.
BACK RIGHT: Representation of *King David* playing a harp from an ancient illuminated manuscript.
BACK LEFT: The *Uilleann* pipes. Eighteenth century.
CENTRE: An Irish-made violin.
CENTRE RIGHT: An example of the Irish Bagpipes.
LOWER RIGHT: Panel showing a harper (King David) on the end of the *Shrine of St Moedóg*. Circa eleventh century. So accurate is the representation that the manner of playing, by pulling the strings with the nails, is clearly shown.
BEHIND HARPER: Specimens of Irish Bronze Trumpets. 900 BC to 350 BC. The National Museum contains a collection of twenty-six of these trumpets varying in length from 18 inches to 8 feet.

Week 2: Sunday

Lent is about scandal.

Rarely is the expression 'giving scandal' applied today, yet it's what Jesus condemns Peter of in the Lenten Gospels. In calling Peter an obstacle in his path, he uses the word 'scandalon', meaning a small stone that trips. We share this accusation of Peter without murmur, for we too have been obstacles or 'scandals' in the path of others.

You are a scandal to me when you are unkind or unjust in the way you treat me. You make me feel small. You damage my self-confidence. You are a scandal to me when you fail to understand my weaknesses, faults, mistakes and write me off as a result of them. You are a scandal to me when you discourage me, keep me down, and humiliate me, when you make me feel inferior. You are a scandal to me when you load me with unjust criticism and sour me with your cynicism. You destroy my ideals, my dreams and blight my hopes.

But you can also be a stepping-stone for me when you give me a belief in myself and boost my self-confidence. When you help me discover the special talents that God has given me. When you challenge me and help me to grow and develop my potential. When you accept me, though others reject, and you refuse to join the crowd who throw the stone of accusation and judgment at me. When you forgive me and liberate me from my past and free me to move forward again, you are a stepping-stone for me.

The question is, will you give scandal today or be a stepping-stone?

Amen.

Week 2: Monday

Lent is about the questions of life.

It will soon be time for mock examinations, a dry run under supervision before the launch. Today, three gospel questions for would-be disciples of Jesus and no passing or comparing allowed:

1. What do we rejoice in?
2. How do we spend most of our time; what do we work at?
3. How Christian is our rejoicing and our work?

Question 1. Do we rejoice in the fact that our name is written in heaven? That we are chosen by God who will protect us through every danger. Or do we rejoice only in lesser things: a new possession, a high grade, a pay rise? Have the tribulations of life, the business and worldly care of each day put God on the back burner?

Question 2. What do we strive at, or who is it that we work for? Do we work for ourselves or for God? Do we strive for our own happiness and contentment or for the works of God: love, care, justice and healing?

Question 3. Will we do this without human tools, protection or security, because this is the only way in which the job can really get done and credit be given where it belongs, to God?

Only three questions, but a lifetime to answer. How are you answering this Lent? That's the real question for today.

Amen.

Week 2: Tuesday

Lent is about believing and seeing.

There are many occasions that could qualify for the title 'personal tragedy'. The doctor says it's cancer; Alzheimers is beginning to rob the one you love of their mind; a stroke takes away your freedom; disease causes you to lose control of your body; a child dies; an accident maims. At some point the question is asked, 'Why me? What have I done to bring this into my life? Common and timeless questions.

In the Lenten gospel one issue is about a man born blind. The question is asked, 'Is he blind because of something he or his parents did?' Jesus answers, 'No'. Sometimes we do reap what we sow, but usually not. The questions Jesus answers are as relevant as the morning paper. It is good to draw some vital truth from tragic times.

1. **Resist explanations:** Sometimes no conclusion is possible. At worst it increases the burden of the sufferer.
2. **Be active:** Ask others to pray for your healing. Look for lessons you should be learning.
3. **Be faithful:** Keep doing what is right.
4. **Be patient:** We see through a glass darkly now, but it won't always be that way. The veil will be pulled back and we will see clearly. Sometimes believing is seeing.

Whatever weighs us down this Lent, let God see it and believe in him.

Amen.

Week 2: Wednesday

Lent is about refreshment within ourselves.

She lived 2000 years ago, from a race few meet, a region most don't visit, from an unfamiliar city. She was a Samaritan woman from Sychar, and yet if we understand this woman socially, psychologically and spiritually we will understand ourselves. What was she like? The letter 'S' best describes her.

Socially she has *separated*, she wants to be alone. We know this by her going to a distant well at the hottest time of the day and year. Why? Well, the second 'S' stands for her condition psychologically. She has *shame*. Shame is a hard word. There is something wrong with us. Shame says I have done something wrong. And the third 'S' describes her spiritual condition. She was *sinning*. The word sin is misunderstood and misused. It simply means to miss the mark; to fall short of a standard. Spiritually like us, she had fallen short. In her case sexually. It might be something else for us: lying or anger or a judgmental spirit or gossiping or over-eating. Perhaps we have given in to some 'ism', alcoholism, workaholicism or something else.

To break this cycle of sin and shame and separation, Jesus literally goes out of his way looking for us. He knows where we are. He knows us and he wants to give himself to us. Jesus is going out of his way to find you and me this Lent. Let him find us. Let the separation and the sin and the shame stop. Let the game of hide and seek be over this Lent.

Amen.

Week 2: Thursday

Lent is about goodbyes.

We find goodbyes difficult, increasingly so as distance divides families. Within frequent reunions a bizarre ritual of gradual separation is enacted as a visit ends. Grandparents, adult children and grandchildren wonder – will it be like this next time? There is chat and silences as the tea is drunk. Goodbye is said in the kitchen, the hallway, the driveway, the car. At long last they are off unless something is forgotten.

Partings are hard because they remind us that life and living means change. We meet and marry, have children, move house, get sick and well again, change or lose jobs, encounter success and failure, see children or friends leave, argue and reconcile, follow our dreams or abandon an old one. We seek to avoid or deny change, but we all go through it.

To anxious disciples at his Transfiguration, Jesus reveals that he is bigger than any changes we could encounter. A 'son of man' of the Lenten wilderness is also the Son of God. Still, human change and goodbyes remain difficult. One day we may realise that the more ancient and authentic meaning of 'goodbye' is God-be-with-you. It reminds us that while miles and situations divide, God always accompanies us. True for Abraham and true for us. So say goodbye to old ways this Lent, but realise more deeply, that even before that, God is within you, before you, behind you, above you, with you and never says goodbye. Wherever you are going God is already there waiting for you.

Amen.

Week 2: Friday

Lent is about how we can handle life.

When doubt is expressed as to our ability to cope with a task or situation, someone somewhere will pose the question, 'Can you handle it?' It combines challenge and concern in a few words. However, Jesus asks much the same question. Handle me and see I am real – an invitation to a floundering Thomas, so far out of his depth, to come closer.

Are you the kind of person who invites people to draw closer to you with all your strengths and your weaknesses, or do you tend to keep them at arm's length? Truer still, are our churches ones that are open and letting people in, no masks or ridiculous religious facades that hide our struggles and shortcomings?

The early Christians sound idyllic and a tad unreal, but every person has battled with the age old challenge of struggling with life, prayer and raising a family and are finding it hard to handle everything. How do you handle what life has presented to you? Like Jesus when he responded to Thomas, let God see your wounds. Let the struggle and difficulties of life not be so frightening that you want to hide them away. A problem shared is a burden taken up from you. Maybe we can't handle things on our own but with God on our side, who can be against us? You see, for us, God can handle anything.

Amen.

Week 2: Saturday

Lent is about facing fear.

There is an old proverb that goes something like this: fear less, hope more; eat less, chew more; whine less, breathe more; talk less, say more; hate less, love more; and all good things will be yours.

It's no accident that 'fear less' is top of the list. It was high also on Jesus' list of priorities. For all his reassurance about not fearing those who kill the body but cannot kill the soul, that to our hair-numbering God our worth is much greater than sparrows – for all this, our guts have this sinking feeling. It's worse when we can't even pinpoint the fear.

Men and women are afraid of a variety of things: that of our families falling apart, of losing our jobs, of not having enough. We fear being robbed or assaulted. We're afraid of sickness, especially cancer. We are afraid of death, our own or that of a loved one.

When these are mentioned, something starts to happen in our gut. Concerns and memories start clicking in our experience. Trust and faith are the only responses. Jeremiah heard the critical voices outside, but he also listened to the One within him who calls to us this Lent. We do well to hear what is said in the dark moments of life. It is only when we face our fear that we can 'proclaim from the rooftops'. Today our fear is the liberation that Lent leads us through. It is the Jesus journey. It is our journey. It leads to joy. When we face our fears we receive the gift of joy.

Amen.

Third Week of Lent

FROM FRONT TO BACK: *The Wash-House* by Sir William Orpen, R.A., R.H.A. (1878-1931), National Gallery of Ireland. *The Blessing of the Colours* by Sir John Lavery, R.A., R.H.A. (1856-1941), Cork Art Gallery. *St Patrick's Close* by Walter Osborne, R.H.A. (1859-1903), National Gallery of Ireland. *Pasture at Malahide* by Nathaniel Hone, R.H.A. (1831-1917), National Gallery of Ireland. *Self-Portrait* by James Barry, R.A. (1741-1806), National Gallery of Ireland. Portion of a Mural Painting by Daniel Maclise, R.A. (1806-1870).

Week 3: Sunday

Lent is about being guilty as charged.

Ireland is awash with tribunals serving a valued purpose in bringing the light of truth to situations. The danger is that we're getting better at recognising public sin whilst ignoring the defects in our own life.

So just suppose a church tribunal was established to investigate … you! The charge? Trying to close the church. The defending counsel skilfully paints a picture of you as a good person: law-abiding, temperate, truthful and a morally good person. You paid your income tax and bills and came to church. You never opposed anything that was good.

The presiding judge at the conclusion of statements and evidence asks you, 'Are you guilty or not guilty of trying to close the church?' 'Not guilty' you plead, 'I didn't do a thing!'

'Guilty as charged,' the judge ruled. Continuing the judge adds, 'You have confessed to the most effective way devised of closing the church, the kingdom of God. You didn't do a thing. You didn't visit the sick, encourage the weak, feed the hungry, welcome the stranger. You didn't reach out to anyone with the Gospel. Perhaps it's because the possibilities for service demands too much from your resources.'

Lent is about doing, as well as not doing. It's about taking a further step on the journey; going an extra mile. It's about the more, it's an extravagant time; the extravagance of love. Be guilty, for love.

Amen.

Week 3: Monday

Lent is about love at first sight.

We understand from babies that seeing takes a while to get used to. Through baby play they learn to sort out the visual data of space and distance and how their bodies relate to other people and objects. Big stuff for a small child.

So what was it like for the man cured of blindness in the gospel, to match familiar sounds and voices to previously unseen people and places? Marvellous, but disconcerting surely. Like a baby he had to learn how to see. Physical sight is one reality, but at a deeper level you see what you are trained to see.

We have all experienced a skilled guide bringing previously unseen depths to a piece of art or building. What are our eyes skilled at seeing? The good or the bad, what's present or what's lacking, a kindness done or the imagined motive behind it? Do we have a view or a vision of people? Religion is no protection from blindness to the hand of God. Family, community, upbringing and ourselves have prepared us to see what we witness.

This Lenten time, pray for the gift of insight. Try to discover what the Lord wants you to see. Your acquaintances won't believe their eyes, but those who know you will remind you that God loved you at first sight.

Amen.

Week 3: Tuesday

Lent is about God going out of his way.

How does it feel to meet someone who knows everything that you have ever done? Vulnerable for one, uneasy and slightly awkward for another. Who could ever stand up to such a scrutiny? But great is the treasure of having as a friend someone who truly knows you, and is still your friend.

It was such a friend that the 'crowd-avoiding' Samaritan woman met at the hottest part of the day. It was like most of the deepest changes in life, a so called chance encounter. His thirst for her life changed a Samaritan woman with a chequered past into a follower. Most of us come to meet Christ in less dramatic ways than she did. However obscure or winding is the path that leads us to some well where we realise that our thirst is deeper than anything earthly could ever satisfy, it is still a good path to take. 'Hunger is good sauce' is a saying that describes how desperate need can make us satisfied with what we have, inadequate as it may be, but Jesus wants a full life, not an existence, for his followers.

'If you only knew what God is offering,' this gospel says. In the gospel, two people went out of their way. The woman to a remote well at the hottest part of the day and God who will always go out of his way to encounter us and offer us a life of renewal. Watch out for God going out of his way for you this Lent.

Amen.

Week 3: Wednesday

Lent is about glory within.

Occasionally television talk shows delight in taking out members of the audience and sending them backstage for a makeover. With subtle and extreme touches of wardrobe, cosmetics and hair style, out comes this no longer just average looking person. The difference can be amazing. The experience is rounded off with a photograph to make the moment last. It is mostly women who are selected. Perhaps it's felt that men are more in need of an overhaul than a makeover, but when we switch the focus from the physical to deeper alterations of personality, communication, leadership and personal attitudes, no gender can be smug.

It is just as well that Lent focuses on more than skin-deep transformation. It is a transfiguration, if you like, of the human heart. That's what the gospel invites – transfiguration. It is certainly not about trying to stay at the points of glory in our lives, like Peter wished. It is more about setting out like Abraham and Sarah. They had a direction, a plan was beginning to unfold, but first an ordinary couple had to leave home and journey to a place not seen, just promised.

That's our journey, to a place not seen, just promised. We get glimpses of future glory to keep us going but not to linger. At times our path is unclear, but the advice, 'Listen to him' stands eternally. Let us listen to God within us, to the God within our hearts this Lent, because it is the glory within that counts.

Amen.

Week 3: Thursday

Lent is about having vision.

Many people have plenty of willpower, it's inner power we lack. This sentiment of not giving in to one's desires seems to go against what society tends to support. The idea is that we should not be deprived of everything we crave.

So, what if you want that fry even though the doctor says your cholesterol was too high? Go and get it at the local fast food restaurant. Getting tired of your spouse, bored? Go out and have a fling. Feeling down in the dumps? Lets get drunk and stoned, to which is added, of course – after all, everybody is doing it.

We instinctively know that not every urge, craving or desire is a worthy one, a truth best illustrated by the account of the son of King Louis XVI of France. His father dethroned, the Prince was taken by his father's enemies. They believed that if they could destroy his morale he would never realise the great and grand destiny that life had bestowed upon him. Over six months the Prince was exposed to everything that could drag him as low as one could slip. And the boy said, 'I cannot do what you ask for I was born to be a King.' Prince Louis held that vision so tightly that nothing could shake him.

As you move through this Lenten time, what vision have you of your life, or yourself? God has great dreams for you, so live well and depend on his power and his will to guide you and give you true vision. Hold God in your heart and know that his inner eye will guide you through these Lenten days.

Amen.

Week 3: Friday

Lent is about being salt and light.

The theme of one of the World Youth Days is contained in the Lenten gospel, 'You are the salt of the earth. You are the light of the world.' As in organising any event, the World Youth Day preparations were like salt and light, imperceptible yet visible.

Like light, the practical details are usually visible, concentrated and somewhat predictable. The spiritual preparation of pilgrims on the other hand is like salt – invisible and at times scattered and unpredictable, yet nonetheless just as vital to the success and life of the event. The human character is much the same. There are visible and imperceptible dimensions to every human soul, but one aim is held by all – making a difference in our world and doing it quietly. But how?

Well, live life to the full: be faithful to your spouse, be the one at the office who refuses to cheat, be the neighbour who acts neighbourly, be the employee who does the work and doesn't complain, pay your bills promptly, do your part and enjoy life. Don't speak one message and live another. After all, I can't hear what you say for listening to what you do – actions speak loudest and like salt and light add flavour and brightness to life.

Add that flavour and brightness to your life this Lent. Let the invisible work of God lead to visible love in your life these Lenten days.

Amen.

Week 3: Saturday

Lent is about the Sign of the Cross.

The Sign of the Cross is the Christian's logo or symbol. From the very beginning, at Baptism, when priest and parent sign a baby on the forehead – to the last farewell, the sign of the Cross over our coffin.

It signifies that the person making or receiving it belongs to the Father, to the Son, and to the Holy Spirit – to the Trinity, in short. Often it's used so mindlessly and indiscriminately that we seldom think of what we are doing. We're too busy waiting for the sermon, the meal, the real prayer that follows, that we don't notice that we have said the most powerful prayer already.

Properly done, in wordless movement it expresses a great deal. You firstly touch your head, dedicating your mind to God, as you say, 'In the name of the Father'. Secondly, you touch the base of your heart, the symbol of love, while we speak the name of the one who loved us first, 'and of the Son'. Thirdly, you move from shoulder to shoulder, from which our arms spring, the agents of action, as we say, 'and of the Holy Spirit'.

With the sign of the Cross, we indicate who we belong to. By this blessing, with this simple sign and these simple words, we show that we are no longer our own man or woman. Whatever follows, the prayer I pray, the meal I eat, the journey I take, the job I do, the journey I start – you do them not in your name or for your glory, but in the name of the Father and of the Son and of the Holy Spirit. You're never alone – three's company. So cross yourself thoughtfully this Lent, and ever this one prayer will envelop you in God's protective care.

Amen.

Fourth Week of Lent

TOP LEFT: Dublin Bowl, in blue and white, made in Delamain's factory about 1753.
TOP RIGHT: Plate in blue and white enamelled pottery. Dublin about 1760.
CENTRE: Ewer, glazed pottery, cream coloured paste covered with a red glaze. Vodrey Dublin Pottery about 1880.
LOWER LEFT: Ancient pitcher, found in a crannog at Lough Taughan, Lecale, Co. Down. An unusually fine specimen of Bronze Age Pottery.
LOWER CENTRE: Specimens of Bronze Age pottery showing incised pattern.
FRONT RIGHT: Vase and cover. Porcelain. Beleek, about 1880.

Week 4: Sunday

Lent is about small kindnesses.

We often remember the names of the first to complete some achievement, be it in politics, business or sport. At Easter we celebrate a woman who was the first to the tomb on that first Easter Sunday morning; the first to see the risen Jesus. She is Mary of Magdala, a long-time friend of Jesus. At the end of the Gospels we know six things about Mary Magdalen:

1. She experienced Jesus casting seven demons from her.
2. She assisted Jesus during a good portion of his public ministry.
3. She attended his death and burial.
4. She went to the tomb on Easter morning.
5. She was the first to see Jesus after he rose from the dead.
6. She announced the Resurrection and Ascension to the Apostles.

Unfortunately, history has not been kind to Mary Magdalen. She has been transformed into a variety of characters, among them the great sinner who washed Jesus' feet. She may never be able to overcome centuries of critical analysis. Yet to have followed Jesus throughout much of his earthly life, being one of a small, faithful group at the crucifixion, and being the first not only to the tomb, but also the first to see the risen Lord, makes her nothing short of a small saint.

Her greatness is in her gentleness. Small acts of kindness are the true definition of greatness. Last to be noticed, but first in God's eyes. Key to the small acts of kindness.

Amen.

Week 4: Monday

Lent is about coming to the rescue.

In some churches the cemetery literally surrounds the church. It is odd and yet fitting to have fewer people inside than outside, with some of the living bearing the same name as their deceased ancestors outside. Cemeteries are good places to gain perspective on life, but, of course, they are awfully painful places too. Overall, our visits tend to be brief and far from lingering.

From the gospel it would seem Jesus isn't particularly anxious to visit the cemetery. He delays for two days after hearing the news of Lazarus' death and by the time he arrives it is four days after the death and immediate burial of his friend. Ironically, the name Lazarus means 'God to the rescue'. While for added measure his home place Bethany means 'house of affliction'. The late arrival of Jesus does not follow the spirit of countless films where the cavalry or rescuer turns up just in the nick of time! But it is real, because for many of us things can seem like that fourth day, just too late.

What we had hoped and prayed for came to nought when illness or crisis changed our busy lives from, 'I haven't the time' to 'I don't have much time.' Not our idea of time in this gospel, but it's God's idea of time. Was this an act of kindness to an old friend Lazarus? Yes it was, and much, much more. An assurance of future glory for all future Lazaruses whenever the green sod covers us. For God is never late if we trust him. He rescues us in his own good time and his time is eternity.

Amen.

Week 4: Tuesday

Lent is about seeing and partly seeing.

In the world of personal communication, making eye contact is held to be important. Along with body language it is seen as an important tool in helping to create a bond between people. We have even brought technology in to assist. That speaker looking soulfully into the camera or at a public meeting could very well be reading an autocue.

However, in Japanese culture, things are exactly the opposite. It is a country where people studiously avoid making eye contact when walking down the street or even in a crowded train station. Why? We are not sure. Maybe it is because of the crowded public spaces in Japan that this unwritten rule has developed to give everyone a small measure of privacy. It is a place where you see but you don't see.

However the Japanese cannot claim exclusive rights on that skill, for it is a technique we have mastered ourselves. We even talk of seeing through a person and in a real sense we have become morally and intellectually blind to what is happening all around us, even though we technically see everything. This Lent let us see truly and let us seek truly to take the plank out of our own eye before we see the speck in our brother or sister. Lent is a time to see God and to let God look us in the eye.

Amen.

Week 4: Wednesday

Lent is about leaving the familiar.

Leaving a destructive situation is never easy. Staying means at least you know what to expect and you can develop ways of coping and keeping your spirit intact. The alternative is an uncertain future.

The enslaved Hebrews expected the lash of the overseers whip, but they knew that at least their food and water was assured. They discovered that freedom doesn't slake your thirst in the desert. It is our story too, fearing hunger, impoverishment, unemployment and social stigma. All too many choose predictability over liberation. It happens in relationships, in jobs, in every area of life. What is predictable may not be healthy, but it is safe.

The story of the Samaritan woman and her unfocused life is ours also. Yet in the heat of the day, when respectable people were under cover, this surprising personal encounter between her and Jesus brims with equality, drowns taboos and flows with dignity. Not bad for a face to face encounter legislated apart by gender and religious practice. A Samaritan woman with a chequered past tried to debate with Jesus as to the best time and place and style for worship, but Jesus told her these issues were irrelevant. She needed more to change her way of living.

In Lent 2012, how will we burst dams, so living water can quench the thirst of our world? What new encounters do we need in order to live the gospel more integrally? Are we prepared to move from the place of 'knowing' to the place of 'unknowing'; to face the unknown in the interests of truth and love?

Amen.

Week 4: Thursday

Lent is about fatal distractions.

The attractions of power, vanity and food are a potent mix in any culture or century, but lest we think that the time of Jesus and our world are unrelated, think again. If the devil were an easily recognisable, repulsive figure, resisting temptation would be no hardship. At the first appearance of pitchfork and horns we would flee up the heavenly ladder.

You see, evil isn't just out there, it is also present in our fears, hatred and prejudices. You don't have to be living in palaces or to be listed among the world's richest people to fall victim to these vices. Take power, for example. Some exert power in their families by controlling everything and everyone. Their prayer is not *thy will*, but *my will* be done. Vanity has a thousand faces; the right look, the right group, seeking people of influence and wishing to be influential. Then there is food. Physical food we all need; enough for everyone's need but not enough for everyone's greed. What do we really hunger for? Love, affection, purpose, appreciation?

In the desert Jesus faces himself squarely without flinching. One thing about the desert is that in a barren landscape there is no hiding place, it is just you and the elements. In a world of comfortless sounds and enumerable distractions, the Lenten invitation to journey is extended to you. It is a risky journey to undertake, you mightn't like who you meet there, outside or inside yourself, but will you head out? It's the only journey worth taking this Lent without distractions. The journey into yourself before God.

Amen.

Week 4: Friday

Lent is about things seen and unseen.

Reading the labels of processed foods can be an alarming experience. Unpronounceable chemicals and strange additive numbers conspire to keep your greens greener and your food sweeter and longer lasting. Among them you will almost inevitably find salt listed.

Salt was served as a currency in some ancient civilisations. When you think that we get the word 'salty' from it, you will get some idea of its importance in the days before refrigeration. It is still used in some refrigeration processes, in dyeing and in the manufacture of soap and glass. Even in making the prisms and lenses of instruments used in the study of infrared radiation, it does its work humbly and anonymously.

But adding salt to a wound, mind you, won't help. Yes, it will keep the wound clean but at a painful price. Healing requires the correct method of bandaging, but fundamentally it is down to good blood circulation. What keeps us from circulating, from being the salt of the earth for others? Just as salt is invisible, this Lenten time let us quietly, almost silently, remove the blockages that keep us from being the persons we were always meant to be. No earthly bypass will do. The road runs straight and true. We must believe in God and we must do whatever he asks of us. Let us remove blockages to Christ in our hearts this Lent and become the salt of the earth for others. Let us be the kind of people of whom it is said – you, you are the salt of the earth.

Amen.

Week 4: Saturday

Lent is about resentment.

A group of doctors were asked which emotions cause the most physical illness. Their answer was 'anger and unforgiveness,' because over time they release deadly toxins into your body. In a strange way their medical know-how echoes exactly the wisdom of our Lenten Scripture: 'Resentment and anger – these are foul things.'

Yet … real forgiveness is not cheap. Total forgiveness is painful. It hurts when we kiss revenge goodbye. It hurts to think the person is getting away with what they did and that nobody else will ever find out:

Logic says: 'Put up your fists.'
Jesus says: 'Fill up the basin.'
Logic says: 'Bloody his nose.'
Jesus says: 'Wash his feet.'
Logic says: 'She doesn't deserve it.'
Jesus says: 'You're right, but you don't either.'

Peter learned that when it comes to forgiveness you leave your calculator at home and love without measure. It is not some saccharine-sweet, limp thing. If it is patronising or glib, easygoing and careless, then it is not the true article. True mercy hurts. So, we may well whimper, 'How shall I forgive others?' We might just hear Jesus whispering back, 'You know, if you never loved, you would never need to forgive.'

Forgiveness is love transformed and deepened. It is at the heart of the Easter story. It has the gravity of resurrection. Journey towards it in fuller measure this Easter time.

Amen

Fifth Week of Lent

AT BACK: Window in the Collegiate Church of St Nicholas, Galway, founded in 1320.
LEFT FRONT: Fragments of the stained-glass windows, thirteenth to sixteenth century, which formerly adorned the Cathedral of St Canice, Kilkenny.
CENTRE: One of the ten stained-glass windows in the Collegiate Chapel, University College Cork.
CENTRE RIGHT: Portion of the stained-glass window *The Last Judgment* in St Brendan's Cathedral, Loughrea, Co. Galway.

Week 5: Sunday

Lent is about call and response.

Our lives are full of invitations to various functions, with responses varying from enthusiastic to reluctant attendance. Despite this, whenever before have so many people lived on their own and in some cases, felt as lonely? The answer to loneliness, however, does not lie in getting others to pay attention to us. The response is to reach out to others. Here are a few pointers to remember when you're feeling lonely:

1. **The best way to have a friend is to be a friend**: If others call or visit less than you'd like, how about calling them? Instead of saying, 'Come and see me sometime,' invite them for a specific date and time.
2. **Maintain a caring attitude towards others**: When talking with others, strive to listen as much as you talk. People will want to be with you if you listen to and care about them, but they will avoid you if you talk about yourself all the time.
3. **Take responsibility for your loneliness**: It is best to be direct with others. Say, 'I feel lonely today, and I just need to talk with you.' This invites understanding. But you create resentment if you say things like, 'I hadn't heard from you in so long.'

4. **Pray for others**: Praying for other people can help you feel more connected with them. Ask others to pray for you too.
5. **Diversify**: Don't rely solely on any one individual for all your companionship. Make new friends. See if there are other people you could phone to help you and they feel less lonely. If you can, get involved in some parish activities.

Remember, your own home may feel safe and secure, but it can become a prison that needlessly cuts you off from others. Open your home, and your heart, this Lent.

Amen.

Week 5: Monday

Lent is about beginning without end.

The film *Michael Collins*, which was about a figure and a period of history within the living memory of many, provoked much discussion and gave food for thought. One question was: Did all these things really happen? If there is controversy about the accuracy of the film on this man and the events of his time which occurred within living memory, what about Holy Week? If we find it difficult to get a clear picture of what happened only seventy five or eighty years ago, what chance do we stand with the events of Holy Week reported to us from the Middle East two thousand years ago?

The slogan 'days and events which shaped our history' is often applied to the period 1916 – 1922. During Holy Week, God paints with a much wider brush as the history of our salvation is mapped out. We will do it with elaborate ceremony, light, words and silence. We do it because there is a lot to celebrate. These are days which shape us and make a huge impact on the way we journey.

If Advent was a time of expectation and anticipation for Christmas, Lent is a time of preparation and promise for Easter and Holy Week before it. At Christmas we celebrated the birth of Christ, at Easter we will celebrate the reason why he was born.

During these current weeks, we move through the central story of our faith. In Lent, we move from despair to hope, from death to life, from sorrow to joy, from beginning to end, or, as we will see on Easter Sunday, beginning without end. Let us continue the Lenten journey now and trust new beginnings in our own lives.

Amen.

Week 5: Tuesday

Lent is about spring-cleaning.

As days get lighter, and the sun becomes brighter, our thoughts turn more to spring. The sun not only starts things growing in the soil outdoors, it also shows up how soiled and dusty things have become indoors. The onset of spring used to be the signal for a thorough spring-clean throughout the house. With modern vacuum cleaners and wipe-clean surfaces, cleaning is not such a mammoth task these days. There are, however, areas that get neglected, places that will look brighter for an extra special cleaning: cupboards, curtains, high shelves and dark corners, all harbour dust and need attention. Most of us have clutter somewhere that needs cleaning out or jobs not done for lack of time or inclination.

The January snow of 2011 in its dazzling whiteness reminded us of what could be called the 'Spring-Cleaning Psalm', Psalm 50, which we hear at Mass. This is a prayer for inner cleansing by a man who knew he was in need of it. David had just been convicted of adultery and of engineering the murder of his mistress's husband. He pleaded guilty before God, 'Have mercy on me, O God, in your goodness and in your great tenderness wipe away all my faults. Wash me clean of my guilt,' he began, and later pleaded, 'wash me until I am whiter than snow.'

God created a clean heart in me. We can clean our houses, but only God can clean our hearts, our innermost selves. Only he knows all about us. He answered David's prayer, and he can give us a thorough spring-cleaning of our hearts if we ask him. Let us ask him in confession this Lenten time.

Amen.

Week 5: Wednesday

Lent is about the visit of love.

My name is Nicodemus. You heard part of my meeting with Jesus in the gospel. I was, or am, I suppose, a Pharisee. The truth was our interest and Jesus spoke with such certainty about God and life that I wanted to hear more. I went by night, carefully even then, for the night has a thousand eyes, but it was worth the risk. It was all good news. I only wish some of my fellow Pharisees came too, but jealousy can blind us all, and to be honest a lot of us were simply jealous of Jesus. Oh, not just his charm and wit, but even more the way he brought God down to people's level. He took down the fence of rules that had been put up between God and people – and with it some of us were sitting on that fence. The people couldn't get over the fence and God couldn't get under it. He introduced people to God. Let people see that God loved them. And he used that word 'love'.

For us it was all very new. Not God the maker, or God the boss, or God the condemner. Not a God you had to be wary of, or afraid of, or suspicious of. You simply can't imagine the thrill of being told that God loved the world so much that he gave his only son. I was there that day too. I was there later on Calvary, quietly as is my way, and I looked and I saw him raised, raised up for all our sins, and I saw him again after Easter. The news was good. The news is good. The news is love, so listen to it this Lenten time.

Amen.

Week 5: Thursday

Lent is about signposts for living.

We don't know the Commandments any longer, that's today's truth. Perhaps not in the sense of having them off by heart anyway, but even if we don't know them by heart, let us try to live the values behind the words, that's the deeper truth.

The Ten Commandments end where they begin. We start with honour due to the Creator and continue with respect for ourselves and all made in his image. We finally reach purity of heart which leads us to where God desires ... to himself. The first three Commandments pertain to the love of God; no idols, no lip service, no Sunday without worship of God. The next four focus on human relationships; to honour our parents, not to kill, commit adultery or steal. They can be reached, in one sense, by reason, as can the last three; not to lie, or covet or envy others.

Yet divine grace is needed to enlighten and strengthen nature. For some, the Ten Commandments in the gospel seem to stress the negatives, what we shall not do, but it is God's love for us that is their essence. Being a Christian means trying to respond by loving God and other people in every situation and in all circumstances. We are to be signposts.

As humanity meets the challenges of the twenty-first century, with problems Moses never dreamed of, the compass of the Commandments still points true north, still shows the way, but the road must be mapped out by each generation as it seeks earthly peace and happiness. That's what we really seek this Lent. Look at the Commandments again and look at them with your heart and you will find peace and happiness this Lent.

Amen.

Week 5: Friday

Lent is about habitual living.

This Friday we realise that another Lent is drawing to a close. What, if anything, are we doing? Will we be any different by its end?

This Lent, decide on what God has called you to be, and then try to eliminate any habit in your life that keeps you from it. Don't just remove bad practices; replace them with good ones. Maybe it's a case of changing Lent from being a time to go 'off' things, to making it a space to get back 'on' the things we have gone 'off'.

Remember Ash Wednesday's threefold call to prayer, fasting and alms-giving. Recognise the enemy that is your bad habit. The defeated Napoleon Bonaparte exiled on the island of St Helena wrote wisely when he said, 'What defeats a man once, may beat him again.' Anyone who has ever lived knows the deep truth of his words. A familiar enemy is the greatest threat.

The enslaved Israelites of the Lenten readings had an enemy with a face. Unlike them, we are free, but the chains of our poor habits are real, with ourselves as the jailor. After all, if you want to know what your life will be like twenty five years from now, write down your seven strongest habits, multiply them by 365 days and then by twenty five years – that's what your life will be like. Are you happy with it? Well, you know what to do. Choose the good habits, repeat your good habits. Just do it, but do it now.

Amen.

Week 5: Saturday

Lent is about the real question.

Ambition exists in our very bones. Men have shown this throughout the ages in so many ways. But it's short-lived. Napoleon Bonaparte, conqueror of Europe and Emperor, died at the young age of thirty-three. Alexander the Great, whose tiny Macedonian army humbled the Persians and even reached the borders of modern India, died at thirty-three years of age.

Tomorrow, within homes we will begin Holy Week with Palm or Passion Sunday. We'll join another young conqueror, a city laid open before him, crowds in admiration. His weapon? Not force as used by Napoleon, Alexander, Caesar, Charlemagne and every would-be empire builder, but love. Jesus Christ founded his empire on love. He died at thirty-three years of age.

It's a week when he will cleanse the temple of the moneychangers, a time to explain about the authority that comes from God. A week where he will admire the heartfelt generosity of a widow who gives all she has. A week in which he will break bread and offer the cup of forgiveness to his little band, knowing they include those who will betray or deny him. Eventually he's arrested, tried, beaten, spat upon, convicted and sentenced to death as a common criminal; his last hours spent in a disused quarry and rubbish dump – Golgotha. His crime? Blasphemy. He dared to say, 'The Father and I are one.' Who does he think he is?

Tomorrow, as we slump into our pews after a perhaps all too familiar story of the Passion, is it time to ask ourselves the same question, 'Who do *you* think he is?' It's an ambitious question but it's the only one worth replying to if the coming week is to see us walk towards our journey's end.

Amen.

Holy Week

TOP LEFT: *High Cross of Muiredach*, Monasterboice.
LOWER CENTRE: Base of the *High Cross*, Tuam. Circa AD 1123.
FRONT RIGHT: Carved panel on the Sarcophagus of King Cormac in Cormac's Chapel, Rock of Cashel.
LOWER RIGHT: Carved stone in Duleek Priory. An excellent example of Irish medieval Sculpture in stone.
LOWER LEFT: One of the carved keystones executed by Edward Smith on the Custom House, Dublin. Eighteenth century.
BACK RIGHT: Carved panel showing introduction of foliated forms, usually the vine.

Palm Sunday

Palm Sunday is about the full picture.

Many adults find that technology eludes them. Even the innocent job of video recording a programme can prove difficult. If you're lucky, you can draft in your average five-year-old to effortlessly achieve that task, otherwise the result is a library of video recordings with labels saying 'beginning missing' or 'ending missing' or 'parts missing'.

In visual terms, Palm Sunday is the sneak preview for Holy Week. No part is left out or missing. Jesus' triumphant entrance into the city on a borrowed donkey. A last supper with close friends. The breaking of bread and the puzzling invitation to do this in his memory. The humbling gesture of washing the feet of his followers. A garden agony, slumbering disciples, the kiss of Judas. Pontius Pilate washing his hands. 'Give us Barabbas,' cry the people.

The scourging and crowning with thorns. The denial of Peter. The way of the cross and crucifixion. The Passion reading leaves us in a prayerful pause at the Garden Tomb.

As we keep vigil this most holy of weeks, it is a time to ponder that there is a part for us all there. We're all capable of betraying him, we've all compromised. We all have reasons for repentance. Holy Week is a time to get the full picture, not just the bits we managed to see. There is need for admission this week. Admission of our own betrayals and the admission of Jesus into our hearts in a new way. It will be hard. But, then, it is the week of Passion.

Amen.

Monday of Holy Week

Lent is about taking up, not just giving up.

Lent is a time to give up, but also a time to take up. For some it may have been a resolution to do the Stations of the Cross during Lent, and if you have not done them so far, begin this first day of Holy Week. Throughout history Christians have longed to literally walk in the footsteps of Christ, but not everyone could travel to the Holy Land so, ever since the Middle Ages, churches and chapels began erecting images devoted to an aspect of the Passion. By the fifteenth century, the Franciscans had developed a devotion they called 'Stations'. It took a while to fix the number and titles of the Stations, but in 1731 Pope Clement XII established the fourteen that we know today. Not that this stopped adaptation. For example, many add a fifteenth station to represent the Resurrection of Jesus. It is as if people were discontent at leaving Christ in the tomb when our faith expresses so much more. Pope John Paul II altered the traditional Stations for his Good Friday service in Rome, as follows, with events from the gospels:

1. Jesus in the Garden of Olives.
2. Jesus betrayed by Judas.
3. Jesus condemned to death by the Sanhedrin.
4. Jesus denied by Peter.
5. Jesus judged by Pilot.
6. Jesus flogged and crowned with thorns.
7. Jesus carried his cross.

8. Jesus is helped by Simon of Cyrene.
9. Jesus meets women of Jerusalem.
10. Jesus is crucified.
11. Jesus promises the kingdom to the good thief.
12. Jesus dies on the cross.
13. The mother of Jesus and his disciples at the foot of the cross.
14. Jesus is placed in the tomb.

Whatever the number or name, the Stations move, inspire and challenge us all to follow Christ through suffering to peace. Just as we all must journey this Lent, through suffering to peace.

Amen.

Tuesday of Holy Week

Lent is about the stories of our lives.

We are reminded in many ways of the passing of time by our diminishing abilities to walk, run and climb, or simply to survive late nights. Among the subtle reminders of age could be the long gospel of last Sunday, of Palm Sunday. Each succeeding Palm Sunday challenges our ability to remain upright for about fifteen minutes. It is a trial that tests honour and physique, with much sympathy from those who fall by the wayside.

In the end, though, it is an age old story. It makes us forget any bodily aches or pains from prolonged standing. It is a fifteen minute sketch of a life, much of which we can identify with. Holy Week begins with adulation. Which of us hasn't enjoyed even a brief moment of happiness and glory? Perhaps all too brief. The story moves on to betrayal. Who hasn't been betrayed or let down? Who hasn't at times been the betrayer promising much and delivering little? And Gethsemane? It might be any place, for who hasn't been alone and frightened and in turmoil? Especially when our closest friends slept on unheeding. And Pilate? Let's not be too hard on him. Haven't there been times when we knew what we had to say or do, but didn't act? And Peter's cowardice, we share without condemnation because we have been there too.

At the end of the gospel we slump in our seats, tired, with a moment to pause to consider the death and see where it leaves him and us; for this Holy Week is about our lives too. We walk in the footsteps of Christ, or at least that's where we are called to walk, over these coming days. Walk with Christ this Holy Week and do attend the ceremonies if you can at all.

Amen.

Spy Wednesday

Today is Spy Wednesday.

It probably says a lot about the mentality of Christians in our part of the world that Lent has much more of an impact on us than Eastertide. The negative over the positive in many respects.

This coming Sunday's gospel redresses the balance somewhat with Mary of Magdala, Peter and the other disciples eagerly running, at dawn, to the tomb on that first Easter morning. Good news in the most unlikely of places, a tomb.

But Spy Wednesday is bad news. Well, has it ever struck you how quickly bad news spreads at national and, of course, even quicker on a local level? Whether the news is about someone's health or woes or failings. Sometimes it descends to the level of gossip. A gossip, as someone said, is a person with a good sense of rumour. How is it that when the topic is positive, the conversation seems to dry up much more quickly? We seem to be almost suspicious about good news, as if we feel obliged to be cautious in our optimism and wary of being too happy. It's too good to be true we sometimes say. Have we ever heard anyone say – it's too bad to be true?

As Christians, we say in the creed every Sunday that we believe in the resurrection. On this Spy Wednesday, can you ask yourself – how deeply do you believe? If the answer is completely then it would fill us with a profound optimism, a secure peace, a courage to face the world and our lives with its strange mix of beauty and pain. Lift up your heads, you sorrowing ones, and be glad of heart, for Calvary Day and Easter Day, earth's saddest day and gladdest day, are just one day apart. Beauty and pain. That's Spy Wednesday, that's today. Will you stay with the bad news, or move towards the good news today?

Amen.

Holy Thursday

Today is Holy Thursday.

Every house with youngsters has chores shared out as equally as possible. It's all part of growing up and taking responsibility.

Shirking happens and is challenged. Undoubtedly, the disciples on that first Holy Thursday night delicately manoeuvred themselves to a position far away from the basin and towel at the door, left for the customary feet-washing. An essential task, but a loathed chore, usually reserved for the lowliest servant. Perhaps some present mentally sussed out who should do the job. Silent thoughts running like – let Philip do it, he has not been pulling his weight recently. Anyhow, everybody sits down ignoring both custom and their own dirty feet. Then one of them rises. It is the King of Kings and Lord of Lords, who rises, goes from supper, lays aside his garments, takes a towel, girds himself and washes feet. Just imagine, the Creator of all things pours water over their feet. Why, he even holds the very molecules of water together, not to mention the lives of his disciples. Hear the silence filling that room. Divinity stripped himself of his garments of glory to cleanse his followers.

That same night, that is tonight, he said, 'Do this in remembrance of me.' Is this what he meant? It's not greatness but grittiness that counts. It is the loving attitude we bring to every detail and encounter that really reflects the spirit of Jesus today.

Today, Holy Thursday is personified by humility, not humiliation. Let us join this harnessing of virtue and humbly wash, and have washed everything that needs brightening in our own lives.

Amen.

Good Friday

Today is Good Friday.

With the forthcoming election in America, we watch as parties attempt to garner votes and build up their candidates vote-catching attributes. But even the slickest of public relations work finds the largest obstacle is actually motivating people to go out and vote, otherwise everything else is in vain.

It is a problem Good Friday doesn't seem to suffer from. Today crowds come out to watch and witness, in all its stark simplicity, the retelling of that first Good Friday. Why? What power has this day on the Christian soul, from 12 noon until 3 p.m.? The wish is to be silent. Somehow we know instinctively that while elections touch fleeting areas, this is serious.

When Jesus cries out in victory, 'It is accomplished,' it strikes a chord in us at our human tendency to stop before we cross the finishing line. We see it in the smallest of things. From half-read books to unfinished letters. From partly-mown lawns to abandoned diets. More seriously in relationship hopping: children abandoned, marriages broken, a cold faith, living in an ever colder world where striving to do good is unrewarded and mocked at times. Are you weary as a parent? Pessimistic about your job or colleagues? Lonely in a marriage? Can't resist temptation? Have you forgotten hope? Weary with doing good? Tempted to quit?

Jesus was, but didn't. As Mother Teresa said, 'God didn't call us to be successful but faithful.' The promise is paradise; no election gimmick to get your vote. It's for those who remain good and faithful servants. So walk on, on this Good Friday. Stay faithful under whatever pain you may have, for tomorrow is Holy Saturday. The day of hope, the day when the church holds her breath in anticipation of new hope. Hold your breath this Good Friday. It is being accomplished at this very hour. It's noontime now … time for us to be silent.

Amen.

Holy Saturday

Today is Holy Saturday.

It is the day when the Church holds her breath. Will all the promises come true or is this the last station on our Lenten journey? It's the day of trust when we hope to move into clarity and new life.

We step out of Lent, with its darker, penitential side, into the brightness of Easter. One of the first sounds we hear is that of running feet. There is the breathless Mary Magdalene grasping her discovery of an empty tomb. Her news brings Peter and John running to the tomb; the younger John ahead of Peter who is handicapped by age and guilt. Peter is the first to enter the tomb, to see and believe. Later downhearted disciples left an unfinished meal at Emmaus to hurry back to tell that they had seen Jesus. Disciples heading back to what they had left, the ungenerous land, the fickle sea, and the ordinary lives that they had left for an extraordinary man.

Running feet bring an urgent message of Easter joy – the Lord is risen! But we live in a time and place far removed from the gospels. It's hard to be joyful when your heart is empty, when you look at an empty chair rather than an empty tomb. Running feet aren't needed when you shuffle in a dole queue. There is no hurry in your day when there is no-one and little to return to, and your days are filled with uncertainty.

But if we believe in the resurrection, we have faith that we are precious to the God who pursues us even into the grave to give us life. All around us are signs of hope: an earth stirring with new life, the seed sown in hope and promise last autumn fulfils its promise. As we move towards this empty tomb tomorrow with our individual emptiness, let us pray that Christ will nudge us awake to hope. In him we have reason for hope, a reason to trust because tomorrow our trust is rewarded with life everlasting. Today is the day to trust. Trust God. Simply trust God.

Amen.

Easter Sunday

TOP LEFT: Lunula of thin beaten pure native gold, engraved with geometric designs. Found at Athlone. Gold torcs found at Clonmacnoise and Broighter, Co. Derry, in 1896.
TOP RIGHT: Shrine called the *Fiacail Phadraig*, fourteenth century. Made to contain the tooth of St Patrick.
MIDDLE LEFT: *The Ardagh Chalice*, composed chiefly of gold, silver and bronze with rich settings of enamel and amber of marvellous workmanship.
MIDDLE RIGHT: The *De Burgo-O'Malley Chalice*.
CENTRE: Silver Tray. Dublin circa 1750. Made by Michael Walsh. Silver cream ewer. Dublin circa 1801. Maker, Joseph Jackson. Silver two-handle Loving Cup. Made by a Cork Silversmith named Caleb Williams.
LOWER LEFT: A *Dish-ring* made of silver plate, sometimes called potato-rings and punch rings. Made in Dublin by William Townsend.
LOWER RIGHT: Octagonal Silver Castor made in Dublin in 1717 by Edward Workman. Silver mustard pot made in Dublin in 1780 by Christopher Haines.

Easter Sunday

Today is Easter Sunday.

Easter Sunday is about a beautiful flowering. All told, the lily might not be the best Easter symbol. It springs up quickly alright, to remind us of the resurrection, but the lily flower also dies as quickly as it rises. Its beauty is so short-lived you barely have time to appreciate it.

Hardly the way of Easter and the resurrection, but that's how many think of Easter, once a year and then back to the old grind. Then again a lot of work goes into growing a lily. It needs shelter, water, food, good soil and tending, a lot like faith really. That particular seed also needs minding. It's one reason why Christians gather every Sunday in memory and anticipation of the resurrection.

The Saturday vigil mass owes its origin to the prayerful night-long watch of early Christians. You see, the resurrection of the body and life everlasting prayed in the creed is so central to faith, it needs time and prayer and reflection to unpack.

They say that there are three questions we all ask of ourselves at one time or another: Where do I come from? Why am I here? Is it really necessary to leave? Most of us wish we didn't have to say 'yes' to the third, yet it is the only answer. Easter Sunday means that because he lives we shall also live. A reason for living and our hope in dying. Easter resurrection happens in small, small ways. We all have small deaths and resurrections, Easter stories to tell, moments of promise and truth, moments of resurrection. Today, tell your Easter story and as you do so, say simply, 'It's good to be alive.' And alive in Christ, means alive forevermore.

Amen.